DON
Santa C
S.   W9-CQT-776

Copy

DON CALLEJON SCHOOL LIBRARY
Santa Clara Unified School District
Santa Clara, California

The Conquest of Mexico

EXPLORATION AND DISCOVERY

EXPLORATION AND DISCOVERY

The Conquest of Mexico

How Hernán Cortés and other conquistadors
won an empire for Spain

Mike Wilson

3 3358 00841 2291

Mason Crest Publishers
Philadelphia

Mason Crest Publishers
370 Reed Road
Broomall PA 19008

Mason Crest Publishers' world wide web address is
www.masoncrest.com

Copyright © 2003 by Mason Crest Publishers. All rights
reserved. Printed and bound in the Hashemite Kingdom of
Jordan.

First printing

1 3 5 7 9 8 6 4 2

Library of Congress Cataloging-in-Publication Data
on file at the Library of Congress

ISBN 1-59084-050-X

EXPLORATION AND DISCOVERY

Contents

The Empire of the Aztecs

BEFORE CHRISTOPHER Columbus and other Europeans arrived in the New World around the end of the 15th century, the Aztec people of central Mexico had built a powerful empire. When the Spanish arrived in Mexico in 1519, they were amazed at the accomplishments of the Aztecs.

Native tribes had lived in Mexico centuries before the Aztecs came. For example, in the southern part of Mexico, the Zapotecs lived along the Pacific coast and the Olmecs lived along the Gulf coast. The Maya lived in the Yúcatan region, and the Toltecs lived in the Valley of Mexico, to the north of these other tribes. The Valley of Mexico actually is at a high elevation—7000 feet—and is surrounded by hills and mountains. It has a system of five large shallow lakes that are connected with each other. These lakes provided water that could be used to *irrigate* crops, or as waterways for travel by canoe.

Farmers in the Valley of Mexico grew squash, beans, *maize* (a type of corn), and other crops. Settlements grew into cities, and thus, the first civilizations were created in the Americas. The Mexican tribes had systems of writing and calculated calendars. In addition, they built great cities. One city, Teotihuacan, was known as the City of the Gods. As many as 200,000 people may have lived there centuries before Europeans came to Mexico. Mexican tribes also worshipped gods to whom they sacrificed animals and some-times even humans.

Many inhabitants of the Valley of Mexico were city dwellers. Over time, *nomads* (tribes wandering without a fixed place or home) came into the valley from the north. These tribes were called Chichimec, or "Dog People." The inhabitants of the Valley considered them barbarians, but the Chichimec were fierce fighters and carried a weapon the people of the valley had never seen before—the bow and arrow. Attacks by the Chichimecs caused many cities to be abandoned. After the Toltecs' capital, Tula, was destroyed around A.D. 1200, Toltecs and Chichimecs in the area settled in new cities they had built along the lakes.

Life as an Aztec

Aztec boys and girls were trained for their future roles in society. Girls were trained to be mothers; boys were trained for combat. When a boy reached 10 years of age, all his hair was cut except for one lock at the neck. He had to wear that lock of hair until he had captured a prisoner in battle. This meant everyone would know whether the young man had proven himself as a warrior.

Aztecs were divided into different classes, or groups, of people. The highest class consisted of the emperor, other rulers, and the nobles. Members of this group had special privileges, such as the right to own land.

Members of the merchant class traveled throughout the empire and beyond. They obtained the luxury items that the nobles desired. They even had the power to declare war and conquer other communities. Like nobles, they had some privileges, but unlike nobles, they had to pay taxes.

Members of the *artisan* class made clothing, jewelry, weapons, baskets, and other useful things from metal, wood, stones, and feathers. Both men and women could be artisans, and their skills usually were learned from a parent who was an artisan.

Most of the Aztecs were members of the lowest class—commoners who tilled the fields or performed other hard labor for the community. The Aztecs also had slaves who did this work for them.

This Aztec drawing on cloth is like a history book. It shows the Aztecs' arrival in the valley of Mexico and their battles against other native peoples of the region. At the center is an eagle holding a snake while perched on a cactus—the symbol they had associated with the site of their capital city, Tenochtitlán.

Fighting continued, however, as the armies of different cities often warred against each other.

It was probably around the year 1325 that the Aztecs came from the north into the Valley of Mexico. The Aztecs called themselves *Mexica*. Like the Chichimecs before them, they were good at warfare. Though they wanted to establish a settlement, the Aztecs were not welcome in the valley.

It is believed that the Aztecs had wandered as nomads for about 200 years before settling in the Valley of Mexico. The Aztecs believed they had been instructed by one of their gods, Huitzilopochtli, to travel to a place where they would see a sign. The sign they were looking for was an eagle on a prickly-pear cactus eating a snake. They must have seen this sign in the Valley of Mexico on the island in the middle of a lake, for this is where they eventually built their settlement. They called the settlement Tenochtitlán, which means "the Place of the Prickly Pear Cactus." Today, it is where Mexico City, the capital of Mexico, is located.

The Aztecs expanded the

> **The state emblem of the Republic of Mexico, adopted in 1823, is an eagle eating a snake. This was also the symbol of the city of Tenochtitlan, the capital of the Aztec empire. Mexico's flag has a picture of an eagle eating a snake on it as well.**

size of the island by dumping dirt and vegetation in shallow areas of the lake, thus creating new land for the island called *chinampas*. After a chinampa was created, it was held in place by posts and then, later, by willow trees. Chinampas were great places to grow a variety of crops, such as maize, beans, chiles, and tomatoes. The Aztecs also fished in the lakes and hunted.

The Aztecs were fierce warriors. Sometimes they hired themselves out as **mercenaries**. Aztec rulers formed **alliances** with and against other cities. Over time, through warfare and alliances, the Aztecs expanded beyond their island home to become rulers over about 15 million people throughout Mexico. By the early 1500s, their capital city had grown to over 300,000 people—a far greater population than any city in Europe at the time. In less than two centuries, the Mexica, or Aztecs, had created a great empire.

Laws were strictly enforced in Aztec society, and punishment was swift. Nobles had to obey the laws just as much as the commoners. In fact, the punishment was more severe if the lawbreaker was a noble. Drunkenness was not allowed except during special feasts or celebrations, although the rule was relaxed for the elderly.

Priests and priestesses were in charge of the important religious ceremonies. In addition to priests, there were "divines" who told fortunes, interpreted dreams, and performed healings. These divines sometimes ate *peyote*, mushrooms, or other intoxicating substances because they thought these drugs would transport them to heaven or the underworld, or would help them to see the future.

Religion was important to the Aztecs. They worshipped many different gods, but the most important one was Huitzilopochtli. The Aztecs believed that the earth had

Huitzlopochtli

Huitzilopochtli was one of the most important gods of the Aztecs. He may have been a great chief whom the Aztecs believed became a god after his death. Huitzilopochtli was important because it was his job to bring forth each new day. Without his help, it was believed that the world would end. The Aztecs believed that each night he chased away his sister, the moon, and his brothers, the stars, and became the sun. Huitzilopochtli was carried up to the middle of the sky, the Aztecs thought, by warriors who had died in battle or been sacrificed at the temple. Then, Huitzilopochtli was carried down as the setting sun by women who had died in childbirth. Huitzilopochtli was very real to the Aztecs, and his work was so important that Aztecs were willing to sacrifice human beings to keep this god "nourished." The name Huitzilopochtli means "Hummingbird on the left."

Human sacrifice was an important part of the Aztecs' religion. This Indian drawing shows a priest holding the bleeding heart of a sacrifice victim aloft to the god Huitzilopochtli. Another victim lies at the foot of the altar.

been destroyed four times previously. It was believed that the present age would end when Mexica was destroyed by terrible earthquakes and monsters came to earth.

In order to keep that day from happening, the Aztecs believed that their god, Huitzilopochtli, in the form of the sun, had to climb into the sky to start each new day. They believed that for Huitzilopochtli to have enough strength to do this important work, he had to be nourished with human blood. This meant that human sacrifice was an important part of the way Aztecs worshipped Huitzilopochtli. Those sacrificed often were slaves or prisoners captured in battle. Sometimes they were children. The Aztec priests would cut open the chest of the sacrificial victim with a knife, take out the heart, and burn it as an offering. The head would then be cut off and held up. The arms and legs would finally be eaten by noblemen and warriors as part of a ceremony. This was believed to give them the strength of their victims.

Blood was important to the Aztecs. It was common for priests, warriors, and even the emperor to pierce themselves in the tongue or the lobes of their ears to draw blood. They believed this self-mutilation pleased the gods. Blood was splattered over the doors, pillars, and courts of temples and houses. The number of human sacrifices increased significantly from A.D. 1430 onward. At a festival in 1487, prisoners were sacrificed at 14 different pyramids over four days. Human sacrifice wasn't performed to be cruel—often, victims were given drugs to ease the pain—but because the gods needed nourishment.

Aztecs weren't just warriors

> **To record their history, the Aztecs compiled books written with pictures. This kind of book is called a codex. Most of what we know about Aztec life comes from the pages of the codices.**

A Strange Prophecy

In the year 1518, strange signs began to appear to the Aztecs. Astronomers saw a comet blaze across the night sky, and two earthquakes shook the Aztec capital at Tenochtitlán. Strange dreams were reported, including one by the Aztec emperor Montezuma's aunt in which she saw men wearing black stone riding antlerless deer into the capital city, destroying everything in their path. Finally, the emperor began to hear reports that strangers with white skin and dark beards had landed in Mexico.

The Aztecs believed that these *omens* indicated that one of their gods, Quetzalcoatl, was returning. According to legend, Quetzalcoatl had left Mexico 500 years earlier, sailing toward the rising sun (east) on a raft. An ancient prophecy said that Quetzalcoatl would return in the Aztec year One Reed—1519 by the European calendar.

The Aztec sculpture pictured here shows Quetzalcoatl emerging from the mouth of a coyote, which represents the earth. There is no doubt that when the Spanish learned about the Aztec superstitions, they used them to their advantage. After  the conquest of Mexico, some Spanish writers even rewrote the legends so they would match even more closely the facts of Hernán Cortés's arrival.

and builders of temples. They were also sculptors and poets. Some of their poetry described their history and their religious beliefs. Other poems expressed the individual thoughts and feelings of the poet about the meaning of life, joy and friendship, death, the glory of war, and other subjects.

Aztecs were also scientific. They studied the movement of the stars and created a precise calendar. They believed in magic and the power of the gods, but they also practiced medicine, identifying herbs and plants that could heal sicknesses.

The Aztecs dominated their neighbors and were proud of their achievements. However, they soon would come in contact with an entirely different civilization—the Spaniards.

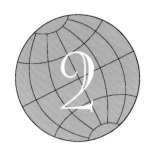

Although Europeans believed that the people they encountered in North America were uncivilized and ignorant, the Aztecs actually had developed a complex society. This is a 365-day solar calendar, which was used to schedule planting, harvesting, annual festivals, and market days. At the center is the image of the sun god.

Mysterious Visitors

DURING THE END of the 15th century and the beginning of the 16th century, Spain and Portugal were actively exploring in the Americas. Columbus had landed in Central America on his fourth voyage across the Atlantic, in 1502. Cuba, Puerto Rico, Jamaica, and Hispaniola (the island that now contains the nations Haiti and the Dominican Republic) were conquered by the Spaniards and turned into colonies during the first years of the 16th century. The Spaniards brought much suffering to the tribes that inhabited these islands. Those not killed by the Spaniards in war were likely to die later from disease or overwork. Spain was also looking for new lands to conquer.

In Mexico, the Aztecs may have heard rumors about these foreign conquerors, the ferocious, bearded white men who were exploring nearby areas. However, there did not seem to be an immediate danger. The Valley of Mexico was somewhat isolated from the Caribbean, where the Spaniards were establishing colonies. The Aztecs were a great people, and they had a great emperor—Montezuma II. They felt that they had nothing to worry about.

Montezuma was named after his great-grandfather, a great Aztec conqueror who had ruled in the middle of the 15th century. Montezuma's father, Axayacatl, also had been emperor. Montezuma became emperor in 1502 and probably was around 50 years old when the Aztecs first had direct contact with the Spaniards in 1518.

As emperor, Montezuma had the best of everything. At meals, he was waited on by many servants and given the best foods. He had jugglers and clowns to amuse him, musicians to play for him, poets to recite for him, and many wives and children. The Aztecs had conquered the surrounding tribes, and he, Montezuma, ruled it all from a capital city, Tenochtitlán, that had never been attacked. Why should he fear stories about bearded white men?

In the spring of 1518, a commoner came to Montezuma's court with reports that "big hills" had been seen floating on the sea off the coast of the Yúcatan where the Mayas lived.

Montezuma II

The ninth Aztec emperor, Montezuma II, was of average height, with wavy hair and a large head. He spoke softly, but was an impressive speaker. He spent most of his days consulting with the leaders of his community. Before becoming emperor, Montezuma had been the chief priest. He also had been a successful general. During Montezuma's reign, he defeated many neighboring cities. He also commissioned many important works of art and rebuilt the capital city of Tenochtitlán after it was damaged by a great flood.

Montezuma was a stern ruler. He believed it was better to make people fear him than like him. When people met with him, they were not allowed to look at his face. This was a new practice that had been introduced by Montezuma. As a result, there were people who served him daily who did not even know what he looked like. Montezuma did not tolerate corruption and was quick to execute those who displeased him.

Montezuma also passed laws that prevented anyone except those of the highest class of nobles from becoming an official or a priest.

King Charles was the powerful ruler of Spain. At his direction, the conquistadors set out to conquer and control all of the lands of the New World. During the early years of the 16th century, he sent men like Diego Velasquez, Juan Ponce de León, and Juan Grijalva to the Caribbean. The king also encouraged expeditions to the American continent, like the one that would be undertaken by Hernán Cortés.

Montezuma sent one of his advisors to investigate. He learned that men in small boats came from these "big hills" with hooks and nets to fish. However, these men had white skin, beards, and long hair. Furthermore, they spoke an unknown language.

Montezuma ordered presents to be made for these strange visitors. He sent them gold and feathered objects, beautiful cloaks, bracelets, and chains. Montezuma's representatives traveled back to the coast and rowed out to the "big hills," which they learned were boats far larger than any boat they had ever seen before. They actually kissed the *prows* of the Spaniards' boat out of respect. They also brought food.

The visiting Aztecs ate with the Spaniards. The Spaniards gave them wine, which the Aztecs had not tasted before. The Spaniards also

> **Montezuma changed his *tunic* four times a day and never wore the same one twice.**

gave them gifts of beads, sweet bread, and hard biscuits. The Spaniards asked the Aztecs about their country and its leader. The Spaniards told the Aztecs they were returning to Spain but that they would come back to Mexico.

Montezuma's representatives hurried back to the palace and told Montezuma what had happened. They showed him the gifts given by the Spaniards. After tasting the biscuits and bread, Montezuma sent the leftovers to a temple in Tula. He had the beads buried at the base of the shrine to Huitzilopochtli in the capital city of Tenochtitlán Montezuma probably hoped that the Aztec gods would be happy at these gifts, and would protect them from the strange newcomers.

In the meantime, nothing could be done except watch the coast to see if the Spaniards came back. Montezuma ordered an artist to paint a picture of the ships that had been seen to keep in the palace records. Most of the Aztec people did not know anything about the strange visitors, so life in Tenochtitlán continued as it had been—at least, until the following year.

FERDINAN: CORTESIVS

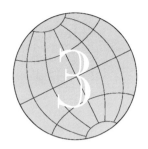

In 1518, Hernán Cortés was chosen to lead an expedition to Mexico. His sponsor, the governor of Cuba, hoped Cortés would return with gold. Cortés was a bold soldier, not worried about riding into the Aztec empire of some 15 million people with an army that numbered less than 600 men.

Cortés Arrives

IN 1493, POPE Alexander VI, the leader of the Roman Catholic Church, said that Spain could have any lands it discovered in the New World if the natives were converted to Christianity. Armed with a religious mission and a desire for gold, Spaniards raced to claim these lands, which is why the Aztecs had seen Spanish ships in the spring of 1518.

On October 23, 1518, a Spaniard named Hernán Cortés was chosen to lead a Spanish expedition to the Yúcatan. His ships, carrying about 530 men, 16 horses, and some cannon, set sail from Cuba on February 18, 1519.

When Cortés arrived at Cozumel on the Yúcatan peninsula, he discovered that one of his captains had arrived early

When Cortés arrived on the Yúcatan peninsula of Mexico in 1519, he ordered his soldiers to sink their ships. Cortés felt that if his men knew there was no way to leave Mexico, they would fight harder to conquer the region.

and, in his greed, had seized food and ornaments from the Mayans, causing them to flee. Cortés eventually persuaded the Mayans to return. He preached to them about Christianity and the sinfulness of human sacrifice. Thus, the Mayans at Cozumel did not try to stop Cortés when he destroyed their *idols*. Cortés had a Christian altar built in their place and put in it an image of the Virgin Mary. A cross was placed on top of the high tower of the main pyramid, and the Mayans put images of the Virgin Mary in their boats. It seemed that conquering the lands would be easy.

Hernán Cortés

Hernán Cortés was born in 1484 in Medellin, a town in the Castille region of Spain. His father had been a soldier. Cortés left home at age 12 to live with an aunt in Salamanca, where he could go to school. He may have studied Latin and grammar to prepare for a career in law (his grandfather had been a lawyer). However, Cortés preferred a life of adventure, so after working as a *notary* for a while, the 22-year-old left on a ship bound for Hispaniola. There, he made friends with important people and got the chance to join military expeditions.

Among Cortés's influential friends was Diego Velasquez, the conqueror of Cuba. Velasquez named Cortés to lead an expedition to Yúcatan, where they hoped to find gold. Velasquez later suspected that Cortés might try to keep the gold and glory for himself. He ordered him not to sail for Mexico. Cortés violated Velasquez's orders and sailed anyway. Thus began the voyage that would lead to the conquest of Mexico.

Cortés was short, bow-legged, and pale-faced. He was an excellent horseman and a good speaker. He was a clever negotiator, cool under pressure, and never lost his temper. He was also very determined to become rich and important.

However, Cortés was in for a surprise.

On March 22, 1519, Cortés moved on to the much-

Montezuma made gifts to Cortés, hoping that would satisfy him and that Cortés would not come to Tenochtitlan. However, at the same time, the Aztec emperor secretly sent magicians to cast spells on the Spanish that were supposed to frighten them. Montezuma hoped the magicians might even cast a spell on the Spaniards to "blow them away." The magicians reported back to Montezuma that their spells had no effect on the white-skinned, bearded strangers.

larger Mayan town of Potonchan. Cortés told the Mayans of the town that he wanted food, and they told him to come back the next day and they would provide it. However, both sides were actually preparing to fight.

The next day, the Mayans brought food, some gold, and jewels. Cortés asked for a basket full of gold. The Mayans said they had no more gold and that the Spaniards would be killed if they did not leave. After a few more days, Cortés confronted the Mayans and read a *decree* that said the Mayans were now subjects of the king of Spain. Fighting quickly began.

The Mayans outnumbered the Spaniards, but Cortés had cannons, which frightened the Indians. Cortés left his horses on the ship—they were going to be his secret weapon. By that evening, the Spaniards had won the battle without losing any soldiers. They then invaded the town.

One reason the Spaniards were able to win so easily is that the Mayans were not trying to kill them. Mayans and Aztecs fought wars to capture, not kill, their opponents so that they could be taken to the temples and sacrificed to the gods.

> **One of the weapons used by the Mayans and Aztecs was the atl-atl. This was a piece of wood used to hurl short, lightweight spears. They also had swords with sharp obsidian blades and bows and arrows.**

The Mayans asked for peace, but fighting broke out again a few days later at a little village called Centla. This time, Cortés brought out the horses. The Mayans were terrified—they had never seen horses before, and thought they were dragons. The battle was a rout. Hundreds of Mayans were killed, while not a single Spaniard was lost. The Mayans withdrew and asked for peace again.

The Spaniards spent three weeks in Potonchan. Among the gifts given Cortés by the Mayans was a slave woman named Malinali who spoke both Maya and Nahuatl, the language of the Mexica. The Spaniards renamed her Doña Marina, and she became a translator for Cortés.

The Mayans did not have the gold that Cortés wanted, but they told him that another tribe inside Mexico liked gold. It was time for Cortés to move on.

Malinali, or Doña Marina

Malinali's father had been an Aztec lord before he died, which meant that Malinali came from the upperclass. However, when her mother remarried another lord and had a child by him, Malinali's mother sold her into slavery.

When Malinali was given to Cortés, she was renamed Doña Marina. She was among the first Mayans to become Christian. Doña Marina was clever, was said to have been beautiful, and was loyal to Cortés. Because she spoke the languages of both the Maya and the Mexica, she was very useful to Cortés. She is known in many history books as "La Malinche." Because she helped the Spaniards against the Mexicans, however, her name also has come to mean "traitor."

The next stop for Cortés and his soldiers was the island of San Juan de Ulua, on the outskirts of the Aztec empire, near where the city of Vera Cruz exists today. (Cortés and his troops later established the settlement that became Vera Cruz). The tribe living there, the Totonacs, had recently come under the control of the Aztecs. Cortés was greeted with gifts, but he only wanted to know about the gold. He questioned the Totonacs about Montezuma and the Aztecs. Meanwhile, alarmed messengers ran to Tenochtitlán to report Cortés's appearance to Montezuma.

Reminded of his previous encounters with the Spaniards, Montezuma sent a *steward* named Teudile with many gifts, including a helmet filled with gold dust and statues and disks made of solid gold. The Spaniards were excited at the sight of so much gold. Cortés told Teudile he wanted to visit Montezuma to thank him personally. Of course, the Spanish leader really just wanted to come and take the Aztecs' gold.

When Montezuma learned

The Aztecs ruled a number of neighboring tribes in the Valley of Mexico. These tribes had to give "tribute" in the form of gold, food, or other things of value to the Aztecs. This was like a kind of tax. Many of the tribes hated their Aztec rulers before Cortés arrived. This would prove to be an important reason why Cortés was able to conquer so many Aztecs with so few Spanish soldiers.

that Cortés wanted to visit him, he was frightened. The Aztecs had heard about the cannon and the horses. In addition, some of Montezuma's advisors thought Cortés might be a god—perhaps even one of the gods that the Aztecs worshipped. Montezuma began to panic and considered hiding. The Aztec people were frightened, too.

Montezuma sent his steward Teudile back with many more valuable presents and food. Teudile also had a message from Montezuema—Cortés should not try to visit him because the road was too dangerous. The emperor sent messengers with presents yet again. This time, Cortés was told to leave. He said he would not do so until he had met Montezuma.

The Totonacs told Cortés they were unhappy being subjects of the Aztecs. Cortés saw this as a chance to turn the Totonacs against the Aztecs by offering to protect them. Cortés headed for the capital city of the Totonacs, Cempoallan, to meet their chief.

When Cortés arrived, the Totonacs blew **conch** shells in his honor. The chief asked the Spaniards to stay. He quickly revealed that he would like it if Cortés would be his friend. Cortés agreed and promised to protect the Totonacs from the Aztecs.

While Cortés was visiting a Totonac town, Aztec stewards came to collect **tribute** from the Totonacs. Cortés told the Totonacs to arrest the Aztecs. Then, Cortés secretly released two of the Aztecs so they would report to Montezuma that Cortés had tried to help them.

Soon, messengers arrived from Montezuma. The gifts they brought included a Spanish helmet, which Cortés had given to the steward Teudile, filled with gold dust. This time, the Aztecs said that a meeting with Montezuma was possible, but that the Spanish should travel slowly because the road was dangerous. Apparently, the Aztecs had realized that Cortés would come no matter what. Also, the Aztecs had learned of the Spaniards' alliance with the Totonacs. They told the Spanish to travel slowly so that they could try and prepare for them.

The Aztecs would not let the Totonacs simply stop giving them tribute. Cortés learned that the Aztecs were forming an army to attack the Totonacs. He quickly sent a large number of his soldiers to fight on the Totonacs' behalf.

The Aztecs appeared wearing feathers and war paint. They carried shields and blew conches. However, at the sight of the Spaniards and their horses, the Aztecs ran away in fear. Cortés now knew that the Aztecs were incapable of stopping him. He also knew it was time to march to Tenochtitlán.

This painting shows the city of Tenochlitán in the middle of Lake Texcoco. The city was founded by the Aztecs around 1325. By the time the Spanish saw Tenochlitán, it had a greater population than any European city. Seven long bridges, called causeways, connected it to the mainland.

The Spaniards Arrive at Tenochtitlán

CORTÉS AND HIS men began the 250-mile march to Tenochtitlán. Montezuma had been telling the truth, however, when he said the road was difficult. Some of the Spaniards became sick and died. In the mountains, the Spaniards ran into the Tlaxcalan tribe. Of all the Mexicans the Spaniards fought, these were the fiercest. Eventually, the Tlaxcalans agreed to be allies with the Spaniards.

When Cortés reached Cholula, the Cholulans seemed nervous. Cortés, fearing they were up to something, captured one of the Cholulan priests and tortured him for information. He learned that Montezuma had plotted with the Cholulans to capture the Spaniards and also had sent

Was Cortés really a Christian or did he just want gold? The answer probably is both. Although Cortés at times was cruel to the Aztecs and the other tribes in Mexico, he did try to convert them to Christianity. At the same time, he saw nothing wrong with taking their gold and making them slaves to the Spaniards— a common practice among many European countries at that time.

some warriors of his own, who were waiting outside the town. Cortés pretended to know nothing of this and asked the Cholulan lords to gather in the courtyard so he could say goodbye to them. When the Cholulan lords arrived, the Spaniards shut the courtyard doors so the Cholulans could not escape. Cortés told them he knew of their plans, and the Spaniards slaughtered the lords and many other Cholulans. Cortés later said that 3,000 people had been killed. Tlaxcalan and Cempoallan warriors who were traveling with the Spaniards then looted and burned the town. Some Cholulan priests killed themselves rather than be captured by the Tlaxcalans and used in human sacrifice. Finally, after two days, Cortés told the Tlaxcalans to stop. Cortés ordered all statues of Aztec gods destroyed and that crosses be constructed and pictures of the Virgin Mary placed in the temples. The Spaniards also took much gold.

When Montezuma heard what happened, he sent

messengers and pretended not to know anything about the Cholulan plot. Cortés continued to pretend that he didn't know Montezuma had been behind it.

Montezuma sent more messengers to Cortés with gold and presents. They said Montezuma was ill, there was no food, and the road was dangerous. They begged Cortés not to come to Tenochtitlán.

During the march to Tenochtitlán, Montezuma sent an Aztec noble dressed as if he was the emperor. The noble was accompanied by magicians carrying expensive gifts. Cortés took the gifts, but was not fooled into thinking that he had met the emperor. The magicians' efforts to cast spells failed again.

However, Cortés was close to Tenochtitlán by now and had no plans to turn back. Montezuma could not stop him.

Montezuma met Cortés on the outskirts of town on November 8, 1519. He was carried to the meeting in a litter with gold and silver embroidery under a *canopy* of green feathers. Nobles walked in front, sweeping the ground before him. Montezuma was dressed in his finest clothes and had many presents for Cortés. Warriors with him wore jaguar skins, and the nobles all wore fine feather headdresses. The terrified people of Tenochtitlán gathered along the roadway to watch Montezuma and the Spaniards march into town.

A supplicant Montezuma greets Hernán Cortés, offering him gifts, in this painting by a Spanish artist. From the time Cortes arrived in Tenochtitlán, Montezuma no longer controlled the Aztec empire.

Montezuma took Cortés and his men to a palace where Montezuma's father had once lived. It must have been very large to house all of Cortés's men—he had about 600 with him. Montezuma led Cortés to a large throne in the courtyard and told Cortés to sit on the throne. The Spaniards were impressed with the size and splendor of the palace. According to letters written by Cortés later, this is some of what Montezuma said to Cortés:

"[B]e assured that we shall obey you and hold you as our lord in place of that great sovereign of whom you speak [the King of Spain]; and in this there shall be no offense or betrayal whatsoever. . . . [A]nything I might have shall be given to you whenever you ask. Now you shall go to other houses where I live, but here you shall be provided with all that you and your people require, and you shall receive no hurt, for you are in your own land and your own house."

Despite the fact that there were hundreds of thousands of Aztecs and only a few hundred Spaniards, the Aztecs were willing to be ruled by the Spaniards. Perhaps they thought the Spaniards were gods, or perhaps they thought the Spaniards were too powerful to resist.

Tenochtitlán was larger than any city in Europe at the time—at least 300,000 people lived there. The Spaniards spent several days seeing the sights of the city and resting. As Montezuma had promised, the Aztecs gave them food,

A *causeway* is a raised road that has water on either side. It is like a bridge, but it is made of land. Tenochtitlán was on an island, but there were causeways that led across the lake.

> At this time in history, Spaniards and Europeans rarely bathed. The Aztecs, on the other hand, bathed regularly and washed with soap. The Aztecs probably thought that these invaders, though powerful, smelled bad.

water, lots of flowers, and treated them very well.

Though the Spaniards were being treated well, they were so few compared to the Aztecs that Cortés decided to take Montezuma prisoner as a way of keeping the Aztecs under his control. This was a very bold move, because if the emperor had resisted, the Aztecs could easily have killed the small group of Spaniards.

Cortés insisted that Montezuma come live with him at the palace where the Spaniards were housed. He and a handful of Spaniards argued with Montezuma about this for the better part of an afternoon. Finally, Montezuma gave in. In fact, Cortés even persuaded Montezuma to tell everyone that it was Montezuma's choice to go with the Spaniards.

Then, Cortés persuaded Montezuma to send messengers to the towns around Tenochtitlán to collect gold and silver as tribute to the Spaniards. Cortés sent part of the gold and silver back to the king of Spain and divided the rest with his troops.

In May 1520, Cortés suddenly had to leave Tenochtitlán and return to Vera Cruz with 266 of his soldiers. The governor of Cuba had sent soldiers to arrest Cortés because Cortés had sailed from Cuba without his permission. The soldiers opposing Cortés were three times as many and were led by Panfilo de Narváez. However, not only did Cortés defeat Narváez, capturing him, but most of Narváez's soldiers joined Cortés's side as well.

When Cortés returned to Tenochtitlán, the city was in an uproar. During a feast to honor the Aztec god Huitzilopochtli, the captain whom Cortés had left behind mistook the celebrations for riots. Nervous, he ordered his soldiers to attack the Aztecs, and some 600 were killed. This angered the Aztecs, who drove the Spaniards back to their barracks. There were only 250 Spaniards and about 8,000 of their Mexican allies against thousands of Aztecs. Cortés brought Montezuma out to speak to the Aztecs. The emperor urged the Aztecs to

Cortés was a clever politician. Several times, some of his troops wanted to return to Cuba or replace Cortés with another leader. However, Cortés always managed to keep control. He was a great speaker and was able to inspire his troops to continue, no matter how hungry or tired they were. He also knew that the promise of gold and treasure could keep troops loyal. It was his promise to share gold with Narváez's soldiers that made them want to join up with Cortés.

The Spanish soldiers are routed as they try to escape from Tenochtitlán in July 1520. This defeat became known to the Spaniards as *La Noche Triste*—the Night of Sorrow.

stop fighting, but the Aztecs refused and the fighting continued.

Cortés knew that the Spaniards did not have enough soldiers to defeat the Aztecs, so on the night of July 1, 1520, Cortés and his soldiers left Tenochtitlán.

The retreat began at midnight. The Spaniards tried to sneak out without being seen.

The way Montezuma died is disputed. In letters, Cortés said Montezuma was killed by his own people, who threw stones at him after he urged them to stop fighting the Spaniards. Aztec accounts, however, say that the Spaniards killed Montezuma.

Most of the soldiers had crossed the four bridges in the city and were about to cross the lake when an Aztec woman going to get water saw them. She sounded the alarm, and the Aztec warriors fell upon the Spaniards.

The attack threw the Spaniards into confusion, and hundreds of Spanish soldiers, along with 2,000 of their Mexican allies, were killed. The Spaniards also lost their cannons, many horses, and much of the gold that they had collected from the Aztecs. Many of the soldiers drowned when they were pushed off the bridge, or causeway, into the lake. The gold that filled their pockets made them sink to the bottom. This night, famous in Mexican history, is known as the Night of Sorrow.

The Founding of New Spain

THEIR DEFEAT ON the Night of Sorrow could have demoralized the Spaniards, but Cortés was a great leader able to inspire his men. He was absolutely determined to conquer the Aztecs. Cortés's troops were greatly outnumbered, but he had an advantage. Many of the surrounding tribes did not like being ruled by the Aztecs and were willing to be allies with Cortés. This was an important factor in the eventual defeat of the Aztecs by the Spanish.

The Aztecs pursued the Spaniards while they were in retreat. Apparently, the Aztecs had decided this was a good time to defeat the Spaniards once and for all. Only seven days after the horrible Night of Sorrow, Cortés and his allies faced over 200,000 Aztec warriors sent by Cuitlahuac, Montezuma's brother and the new leader of the Aztecs. The battle took place at Otumba, northeast of Tenochtitlán.

At first, it appeared that the Spaniards could not win. There were many more Aztecs than Spaniards, and the Spanish soldiers were tired and hungry. Many of them were also wounded from previous battles. Cortés realized that he needed to do something dramatic or the Spaniards would lose.

Cortés noticed a group of Aztec captains wearing splen-

This native drawing of the battle of Otumba shows the Spaniards' attack on the Aztec leaders. Cortés's strategy gave the advantage to the Spanish soldiers and their allies, enabling them to defeat a much larger force.

did feathered costumes. He decided to attack these leaders directly. He and five other soldiers on horses charged

> **Cortés claimed to have lost two fingers in the battle of Otumba.**

through the Aztec soldiers, headed straight for the Aztec leaders, and killed them, throwing the Aztec soldiers into confusion. The Spaniards had won.

Cortés now made his way toward the mountains of Tlaxcala. The Tlaxcalans had been allies with Cortés and had helped sack the town of Cholula. However, the Aztecs sent messengers to the Tlaxcalans and urged them not to help the Spaniards this time. The Tlaxcalans debated among themselves about which side to take.

When Cortés arrived, the Tlaxcalans said they would help the Spaniards under certain conditions. Among the promises Cortés made to them was that the Tlaxcalans could have the town of Cholula, share in the spoils of war, and never have to pay tribute to the Spaniards. In return, the Tlaxcalans agreed to take the side of the Spaniards. The Tlaxcalans would prove very important to Cortés.

> **Cortés was lucky that the Tlaxcalans were willing to fight on his side. The Spaniards were wounded and weak, and the Tlaxcalans could easily have killed them all, changing history dramatically.**

Cortés and his soldiers began a campaign to conquer towns outside Tenochtitlán. The campaign would prove to be brutal. The first battle was at Tepeaca, about 40 miles southwest of Tlaxcala in August 1520. About 500 Spaniards and 2,000 Tlaxcalan warriors captured the town of Tepeaca.

Cortés has been criticized for letting his Mexican allies practice cannibalism and human sacrifice. In his determination to conquer Mexico, Cortés must have thought it was necessary to look the other way so that his allies would continue to help him. Later, the Spanish would prevent Aztecs and other native tribes from practicing cannibalism and human sacrifice.

After winning, Cortés and his soldiers continued to kill some of the Tepeacan men. The women and children were made slaves, branded on their cheeks, and sold for 10 pesos. Many Tepeacans were also carried off by Tlaxcalans to be sacrificed and eaten.

This pattern was repeated in other towns in the Mexico Valley. Many other towns, hearing about what Cortés and his allies did to those who resisted, simply gave in without a fight.

While Cortés and his allies seized control of the countryside town by town, the Aztecs and other Mexican tribes were experiencing another tragedy—*smallpox*. The Spaniards carried with them the smallpox virus. Because there had been many epidemics of smallpox in Europe, most of the Spaniards had built up immunity to the disease. However, the Mexicans had never been exposed to the disease before. Entire Mexican towns were wiped out by smallpox. In some places, there weren't even enough healthy Mexicans to gather the harvest.

Cortés and his soldiers took control of Texcoco, a lakeside town not too far from Tenochtitlán, without any opposition. The reason there was no opposition is that the people living there were afraid of the Spaniards, as were many of the tribes. Using this town as a base camp, the Spaniards attacked Iztapalapan 20 miles away. Chiefs from other lakeside towns began coming to Cortés and offering to be allies.

The Aztecs sent messengers to the other towns, urging them to remain loyal to the Aztecs. However, these towns had been unhappy under Aztec control and they resented the Aztecs. One by one, towns came under the control of the Spaniards, either through battle or because their chiefs offered to ally themselves with Cortés.

> **"Conquistador" was the name given to the Spanish conquerors of lands in the Americas.**

Cortés began to prepare for his assault on Tenochtitlán. Part of his plan of attack involved using boats, which he had his men begin building.

The Aztecs thought that disease was sent as a punishment by the gods. The fact that the Spaniards did not get smallpox made them seem even more like gods to the Aztecs and made it seem that the Spaniards were destined to win.

Meanwhile, things were not going well for the people in Tenochtitlán. Smallpox was spreading inside the city, and many of the Aztecs, including Cuitlahuac, the new Aztec emperor, died. The Aztecs chose Cuauhtemoc, a fierce warrior and a nephew of Montezuma, to lead the Aztecs in the defense of Tenochtitlán.

It was now spring in 1521.

Part of Cortés' plan was to blockade the city of Tenochtitlán and cut off all food and supplies. To do this, Cortés needed to control the lake that surrounded the island town of Tenochtitlán. Therefore, boats were very important.

The boats, called "brigantines," were built a mile and a half away from the lake so that the Aztecs, patrolling the lake in their canoes, would not interfere. Since the boats were being built inland, a channel about 12 feet deep and 12 feet wide had to be dug from the place where the boats were built to the shore of the lake. This way, when the boats were ready the channel could be flooded with water and the vessels could be sailed out into the lake.

On April 28, 1521, 12 brig-antines were launched. Each was able to carry 25 to 30 men plus a cannon.

Cortés asked his allies to supply warriors to help him.In letters he later wrote, Cortés claimed he had an army of about 150,000 warriors

Cuauhtemoc was only 18 years old when he was chosen to lead the Aztecs. He was a brave leader, well respected by both the Aztecs and the Spaniards. His name means "Descending Eagle."

The Aztecs were trapped inside Tenochtitlán. Cortés destroyed the *aqueducts* that supplied water to the city, and Cortés soldiers patrolled the lake in the boats they'd built. During May and June, the Spaniards fought the Aztecs. The Aztecs were starving, and the Spaniards had more allies, but the Aztecs held on. Cortés continued to attack them both from land and by sea.

Finally, on June 30, 1521, Cortés ordered a full attack on Tenochtitlán with his combined forces. A sudden counter-attack allowed the Aztecs to capture a number of Spaniards, however, and Cortés had to retreat.

Late that afternoon, two of Cortés's captains came across Aztec warriors carrying the severed heads of the Spaniards they had executed. The Aztecs flung the heads at the Spaniards, shouting threats. About that time, a great noise of drums and trumpets sounded. This was the Aztec signal

This drawing of Spanish soldiers killing Aztecs inside a temple is taken from a 1579 book about the Spanish conquest of Spain titled *History of the Indians*.

that a sacrifice was about to take place. Since the sacrifices took place on top of high temples, everyone in Tenochtitlán could see what was happening.

Cortés and his men watched helplessly as the captured Spaniards were taken up the stairs of a temple and stretched across the stone. The Aztec priests cut out the hearts of the Spanish prisoners while they were still alive. Cortés and his soldiers retreated. This defeat caused many of Cortés's Mexican allies to abandon him. It appeared, at least for a while, that the Spaniards might be defeated after all.

For the next four days, the Aztec celebrations and sacrifices continued while the Spaniards stayed in their camp.

Cuauhtemoc sent messengers to nearby Mexican tribes, urging them to take the side of the Aztecs. He also sent the heads, feet, and hands of the Spaniards they'd killed and several horse heads as well. He wanted to show the other native tribes that the Spaniards could be defeated and that the Aztec god, Huitzilopochtli, would win. However, Cortés had sent soldiers to help some of these Mexican tribes in battles against their enemies, and this kept some of Cortés's allies from abandoning him.

In the meantime, the Aztecs did not attack Cortés. By the middle of July, Cortés decided that the Aztecs had suffered so much from the warfare, *famine*, and disease that they could not possibly hold out much longer. The Spaniards still controlled the lake, and their Tlaxcalan allies were coming back. Also, more soldiers, weapons, and gunpowder were sent from Spain.

The Spaniards continued to attack, and the Aztecs could not hold them back. The Spaniards had victory after victory during the last two weeks in July. Soon, Cortés controlled three-fourths of the city. Cortés burned down all of the homes and temples in Tenochtitlán. Thousands died on both sides,

When Cuauhtemoc started running out of warriors, he began to dress women for fighting, something Aztecs had never done before.

Two of Montezuma's sons led a group of Aztec nobles who wanted to negotiate with the Spaniards, but Cuauhtemoc had all of them executed. He refused to surrender to the Spaniards.

but still Cuauhtomec would not surrender.

On August 13, 1521, Cortés marched into the city again. Most of the Aztecs surrendered without a fight this time. They were exhausted and starving. Many of the Aztec leaders were fleeing in canoes, taking with them their gold, women, and children. One of the Aztecs caught fleeing was Cuauhtemoc. He was brought to Cortés, who spared his life.

After their defeat, the Aztecs were ordered to leave their city. There may have been as many as 240,000 dead inside the city of Tenochtitlán. The Spaniards began to clear the city and used Mexican laborers to build new homes for the Spaniards inside Tenochtitlán. Cortés renamed the city Mexico. The center of the Aztec empire now belonged to the Spaniards.

The Spaniards did not find as much gold in Tenochtitlán as they had hoped. In fact, very little was left to divide among the soldiers. Though some gold and silver had been found, the great treasure of Montezuma that Cortés believed existed never was found. The Spaniards had to settle for land instead.

Cortés' captains and future settlers of "New Spain," the name given by the Spaniards to the lands Cortés had conquered, received large grants of land. They also received Mexican workers with the land who were little more than slaves. Life was hard for the Aztecs remaining in New Spain.

Priests now began to arrive in New Spain. They generally treated the Mexicans better than their Spanish rulers and tried to convert them to Christianity. Old Aztec temples and statues of Aztec gods were destroyed.

This native drawing on cloth shows Spanish priests converting Indians in New Spain. Many Aztec buildings, statues, and books were destroyed because they went against Christian teachings.

Although the arrival of the Spanish destroyed the Aztec culture, some reminders of their civilization remain today, such as the El Castillo pyramid in Chichén Itza.

Instead, Aztecs were required to adopt the customs, religion, and language of the Spaniards. Over time, Spaniards and Mexicans would marry, and the future citizens of Mexico would be a mixture of European and native Mexican blood. Cortés himself had a child by Doña Marina, the Mayan translator who had helped him conquer Mexico.

Cortés became governor of New Spain. However, when he left on another expedition to what is now Honduras, other Spaniards in Mexico City began to plot to take power away from Cortés. When he went back to Spain and met with the king, Cortés was treated well and honored, but the king did not entirely trust him. He remembered how ruthless Cortés had been in dealing with the governor of Cuba, Diego Velasquez, and his lieutenant Panfilo de Narváez, and he suspected that the conquistador had not always given his fair share of gold to the royal treasury. So the king refused to reappoint Cortés as governor of New Spain.

Cortés eventually became bored in Mexico. After more adventures in other parts of the world, Cortés fell ill in Spain and died on December 2, 1547, at the age of 63. His bones were taken back to New Spain and buried in the country he founded, now called Mexico.

There are no monuments to Cortés in Mexico. However, no one can deny that he and a small group of Spaniards managed to conquer one of the great empires of their time, significantly shaping the future lives of the people of Mexico.

Chronology

1325 The Mexica, or Aztecs, settle on an island in the Valley of Mexico; the site of their settlement would become the city of Tenochtitlán, the capital of the Aztec empire.

1484 Hernán Cortés is born in Medillin, a town in the Castille region of Spain.

1502 Montezuma II becomes emperor of the Aztecs.

1518 Montezuma's representatives meet with Spaniards whose boats have landed on the coast; this is the first direct contact between the Spanish and the Aztecs.

1519 On February 18 Cortés sets sail from Cuba for Mexico; in March the Spaniards have their first battle with Mayans at Potonchan, defeating them without losing a single soldier; on November 18, after marching through Mexico with little serious opposition, Cortés arrives at the outskirts of Tenochtitlán, where he is met by Montezuma.

1520 In May, Cortés and his men defeat a larger Spanish army, commanded by Panfilo de Narváez, which has come to arrest Cortés; on July 1, Cortés and his soldiers are driven out of Tenochtitlán and many Spaniards die during the "Night of Sorrow"; on July 8, Cortés's troops defeat a large group of Aztec warriors sent to pursue the Spaniards.

Chronology

1521 On August 13, after a long siege, Cortés and his Spanish soldiers, along with their Mexican allies, march into Tenochtitlán; they capture the Aztecs' leader, Cuauhtemoc, who was trying to escape in a canoe; Tenochtitlán surrenders to the Spaniards.

1547 On December 2, Hernán Cortés dies in Spain at the age of 63.

Glossary

alliance—an agreement by two or more groups to work together for a common goal.

aqueduct—a canal made to carry a large amount of flowing water.

artisan—a person who practices a particular craft.

canopy—a cloth covering carried above a person of high rank.

causeway—a raised path or road over water.

conch—a sea animal with a large spiral shell.

decree—an order usually having the force of law.

famine—a severe shortage of food resulting in widespread hunger and starvation.

idol—a symbol of an object of worship.

irrigate—to bring a supply of water to a dry area, especially in order to help crops to grow.

maize—a type of corn that was cultivated by the Native Americans of Mexico before the arrival of the Spanish.

mercenary—a person who is paid to be a soldier.

nomad—somebody who wanders from one place to another.

Glossary

notary—a public officer who certifies writings and makes them authentic.

omen—a sign that is believed to warn about a future event.

peyote—a drug made out of dried cactus.

prow—the front part, or bow, of a ship.

smallpox—a contagious disease characterized by pustules, skin eruptions, and scarring.

steward—a person hired to work in a large household or estate to manage finances, servants, and other matters.

tribute—a payment made by a ruler or state as a sign of submission to another ruler or state.

tunic—a knee-length outer garment worn belted at the waist.

Further Reading

Berdan, Frances F. *The Aztecs of Central Mexico, An Imperial Society*. Fort Worth, Texas: Harcourt Brace Jovanovich, 1982.

Carrasco, David, and Scott Sessions. *The Aztecs: People of the Sun and Earth*. Westport, Conn.: The Greenwood Press, 1998.

DeAngelis, Gina. *Hernando Cortés and the Conquest of Mexico*. Philadelphia: Chelsea House, 2000.

Thomas, Hugh. *Conquest: Montezuma, Cortés, and the Fall of Old Mexico*. New York: Simon and Schuster, 1993.

Warburton, Lois. *Aztec Civilization*. San Diego: Lucent Books, 1995.

Hunter, Amy Nicole. *The History of Mexico*. Philadelphia: Mason Crest Publishers, 2003.

Internet Resources

The Spanish conquest of Mexico

http://www.pbs.org/opb/conquistadors/mexico/adventure1/a5.htm

http://www.umich.edu/~proflame/texts/mirror/conflict.html

Aztec Accounts of the Spanish conquest

http://www.ambergriscaye.com/pages/mayan/aztec.html

http://www.humanities.ccny.cuny.edu/history/reader/Cortés.htm

Index

Photo Credits

page
6: Corbis Images
10: Mary Evans Picture Library
14: Scala/Art Resource, NY
16: Werner Forman/Art
    Resource, NY
18: Mary Evans Picture Library
21: Archivo Iconographico,
    S.A./Corbis
22: Gianni Dagli Orti/Corbis
24: Scala/Art Resource, NY
26: Bettmann/Corbis

34: Charles and Josette
    Lenars/Corbis
38: Giraudon/Art Resource, NY
42: Hulton/Archive/Getty Images
44: Archivo Iconographico,
    S.A./Corbis
46: Hulton/Archive/Getty Images
52: Giraudon/Art Resource, NY
55: Hulton/Archive/Getty Images
56: Corbis Images

Front cover: Hulton/Archive/Getty Images
Back cover: Scala/Art Resource, NY; Corbis; Giraudon/Art Resource, NY

About the Author

Mike Wilson has published articles on history in magazines for children. He also has written instructional material for Harcourt Brace and will have a biography of Father Roy Bourgois published by John Gordon Burke Publishers.